# *Healing*
## *Spirit, Soul, and Body*

FINDING GOD
IN THE MIDST OF EVERYDAY LIFE

George and Betty Jackson

Cover & interior design: Buckinghorse Design, Nashville
First printing: 2010
ISBN: 978-1-61718-000-2

Printed in the United States of America

# Contents

**A Note of Explanation:**

As you read through this booklet, you will find questions. Please take the time to answer each question in the blanks provided. When you see this symbol,

keep the answers hidden with a card or piece of paper until you've filled in the blanks. You will find immediate feedback as the answers are listed right below the questions. If you answer the questions before reading the answers provided, you will receive more help from the booklet. It takes just a few minutes to work through the booklet and by spending this time, you will find out how to follow God as He heals your body and changes your life.

# Foreword

It is often said, "If you have your health, you have everything." When God made provision for His people, He addressed our spiritual and physical well-being. God's mercies truly are "new every morning" (Lamentations 3:23).

This booklet is intended as a tool to invite you toward God's best for your life—body, soul, and spirit. The wonderful truth of God's Word is a beacon of light directing us toward a transformed life.

These pages contain biblical principles that have been lived out; the message here is not just theological supposition. I have observed the potential of trusting God in the lives of my parents and in the lives of thousands of people with whom they have shared these truths.

As you read these pages, open your heart. God has a purpose for your life, a plan for your good. God will never limit your potential. Break through to belief in a new way.

Allen Jackson
Senior Pastor
World Outreach Church

# Introduction

This book is written to share with you some of the biblical truths that we have learned along the path of our earthly journey. The passages of Scripture contained herein have been a tremendous comfort to us in our day-to-day struggles as we have faced various kinds of sicknesses, diseases, and disappointments; in fact, they were often answers to questions we did not know we had. What does God say about our health? Does He notice? Does He care? Will He help us?

"Yes" is the answer in all things! This is not an in-depth study but a small tool to be used when you are healthy and have no problems as well as when trouble comes and you need answers. Many times we have sat alone in our own home, quietly in the still of night, when our faith was shaken by what we felt in our own bodies coupled with a diagnosis given by a most trusted physician. We have found ourselves suddenly in a doctor's office for ourselves, with a family member, with a friend, or in a hospital room knowing there were grave possibilities ahead. Pondering the great truths of God's Word has been our greatest hope, often to find a diagnosis change, or a medical solution put forth, thereby instantly removing the fear that gripped our hearts.

Wherever Betty and I have gone in the world, we have found individuals who have faced the same trials and experienced the same victories. We are both survivors: Betty has survived breast cancer, and I have survived prostate cancer. We share here a part of our journey and some of the obstacles to healing that we encountered. The Bible is a plan for healing of physical, spiritual, and emotional needs, leading to freedom from addictions and forgiveness for others and ourselves.

We are not products of a seminary, a Bible school, or even an online Bible course. Though we would be happy to have any of those credentials, we met Jesus at the point of our need and found Him to be very reliable. It was in the marketplace, in the midst of a busy equine practice, where we learned to trust Him. It was in the veterinary clinic that we learned to tell others. Eventually we became the founders of World Outreach Church. Now there are thousands in both the church and the business world who are sharing their faith.

The church of Jesus Christ is made up of people from every tribe, every tongue, and every nation. Each of us comes with our own life experiences. But we must all, in humility, find our way to one place, the cross of Jesus. Wherever you may be in the world, whether in a tiny bamboo hut in a warm climate or in a palace in Europe, we trust we will travel the same road. And one day, with the Holy Spirit as our guide, with the constant love of that great Shepherd of the sheep, the Lord Jesus Christ Himself, we will arrive safely in the presence of God for all eternity.

George A. Jackson, DVM
Founder, World Outreach Church

# CHAPTER ONE

# Jesus Changes Everything

······································

The air was fresh; spring flowers were in bloom. The streets were lined with pink and white blossoming dogwood trees as I drove myself to Boone County Hospital in Columbia, Missouri. George had left a couple of hours earlier for the campus where he would sit for national boards at the University of Missouri's School of Veterinary Medicine. We had spent five years in Columbia. In just one month George would be graduating. Allen was seven years old, and Phillip was nearly three. Doyle was to be born the following morning.

I had been in and out of the hospital for the past month. Phillip had been with my parents and my sister, Glenda, in southern Missouri. Meanwhile, George and Allen were both in school each day in Columbia. Once settled in a room at Boone County Hospital, the surgeon entered the room and gave me the news that tests had confirmed that I had breast cancer and would need radical surgery after the C-section I was scheduled for the following morning. This was no great surprise to us since I had had breast problems since I was eighteen. In each pregnancy the danger increased.

Late that evening, George and three physicians arrived at my room. The doctors explained to George why they felt it absolutely necessary to have our permission to do whatever surgery they needed to do once the baby arrived. The doctors insisted that without surgery I had no more than six months to live. George refused to give them permission, saying, "I would not do that to a cow, and I will not allow it for Betty." Sitting in the bed listening to the conversation, I was thinking, *I am no cow*. I must say, I never doubted that George's decision was the best for me. The physicians left the room. We had a few minutes together. Then the lights were out. I was left alone.

As I sat quietly thinking, I realized that *I did not know where I would spend eternity*. I had gone to church all my life. In the months preceding this time, as we drove through the streets on our way to the Methodist church we attended, I would see the beautiful architecture of the church buildings on street corners and would think to myself, *Why are we so divided; why can't we be one?*

George's mother had died when he was only a few days old. I knew that as a father himself, he still missed the mother he never had. We lived with the fact that a child is left with a gaping hole in his heart after losing a parent. This fact was foremost in my mind.

When Doyle Aaron was nine days old, we flew to Rochester, Minnesota, to the Mayo Clinic where I was scheduled for surgery. While we waited to board the plane in Kirksville, Missouri, where George's parents lived, we stood together with Allen and George's father. Allen squeezed my hand. As I looked down at his little face he said, "Mommy, please hurry. I can't make it much longer without you."

Once we were in the air and above the clouds, I said a prayer: "If there is a God, please let me know the truth before I die so that I might tell it to my children." Should we be Methodist, Baptist, Catholic, or Jewish? Allen was only seven years old, but I felt if I told him, "When you grow up, be a Catholic, a Methodist, or a convert to Judaism," he would believe what I told him, and he would in turn tell his brothers. We arrived at the Mayo Clinic. Then, after two full days of examinations it was determined that I had no cancer.

One month later, after George had graduated, we moved to North Miami Beach, Florida, where he had taken a job with his choice of equine veterinarians across the nation. We went immediately to the Hollywood Hills Methodist Church, where we met an airline pilot who taught us that we must know Jesus as our personal Savior. We knelt at the coffee table in his living room and said a simple prayer that changed the entire course of our lives:

> I believe that Jesus Christ is the Son of God, that
> He died on the cross for my sins. I am a sinner, and
> I need a Savior. Lord Jesus, come into my heart; be
> the Lord of my life.

A few days after that, I had just given the children their lunch and was cleaning up the kitchen. With dishcloth in hand, I heard these words through the ceiling of the kitchen: "You said." I looked up to the ceiling, from which the voice continued, "You said, 'Let me know the truth before I die.'"

I replied, "Yes, I did say that." The voice said, "I am the Truth!" I ran to my Bible and opened it to **John 14:6: "I am the way and the truth and the life. No one comes to the Father except through me."**

Then I knew. The truth was not whether I was a Baptist, Methodist, Catholic, or Jewish, but whether or not I knew Jesus as my personal Savior. I knew one could profess any of those religions and still not know Him.

## FIVE YEARS CANCER-FREE

In the spring of 1970, I began to discover lumps in my body. I did not want to tell George. However, when "Aunt Mary," a strong Christian friend who had been a missionary to Cuba at the time of the Castro takeover, arrived at our house, we knew we had to do something. At her urging, I entered Miller Clinic in Nashville and had breast surgery. The lumps were diagnosed as "diseased tissue." When I left the hospital, I asked the attending physician about it. He replied simply, "You are what we call 'high risk,' and there is nothing you can do to prevent it."

Two weeks later, I had lumps back again for the third time and was overwhelmed with fear. I called two physicians, one in Kansas City who had delivered our first two sons, and Dr. Bill Reed, a prominent Christian surgeon practicing in Florida. They each recommended immediate surgery. But after I hung up the phone, feeling extremely discouraged, I walked out onto the patio and I heard these words: "What I gave you by grace, I want to teach you to walk out by faith."

It was near this time that Derek and Lydia Prince visited us in Tennessee. As they were leaving to return to Florida, I asked

Lydia to pray for me. She looked into my eyes and replied, "Betty, until you overcome fear, I will not pray for you." Her wise response sent me to the Word of God. I chose a Bible from our shelf and in the next few months made my way slowly through the New Testament, marking the passages that I thought described myself.

First of all, I learned that I really did not know what the Bible said about healing. In reading through the New Testament, it became clear to me that Jesus died not only for our sins but for our sicknesses.

Second, I came to see there were two forces at work in my life: God, who was good; and Satan, who was evil. While each had a plan, I became determined to choose God with all my heart.

Third, He had said, "What I gave you by grace [which was healing], I want to teach you to walk out by faith." If He is willing to become our teacher, we must make the decision to become His student. Slowly faith comes. The process continues until we will someday see Him face-to-face.

# CHAPTER TWO

# The Word of God: An Unmatched Power

**Hebrews 4:12 NKJV:**

> The word of God is living and powerful, and sharper than any two-edged sword, piercing even to the division of soul and spirit, and of joints and marrow, and is a discerner of the thoughts and intents of the heart.

## Describe five characteristics of the Word of God:

1. _____

2. _____

3. _____

4. _____

5. _____

**Answers:**

1. Living
2. Powerful
3. Sharp
4. Pierces soul, spirit, joints and marrow
5. Discerns the thoughts and intents of the heart

The author of Hebrews describes the Word of God as a living power that judges as with an all-seeing eye, penetrating a person's innermost being, *soul and spirit, joints and marrow*. This is the totality and depth of one's being. If we allow it, God's Word will convict us of wrong and teach us what is right.

It is good to know that when you read God's Word, God's Word is reading you.

You are given an opportunity to change with a simple prayer:

**Faith's Response:**

Heavenly Father, I know I am wrong in this area of my life:

_____

Please help me to change in thought and action. In Jesus' name, amen.

# GOD'S WORD IS ALIVE AND POWERFUL

I was born with the disease cystic fibrosis. I could have easily allowed it to overcome me. Through surrendering my life and my health to the Lord, I found His continued healing. With my life expected not to reach beyond two years of age, I have since realized that God had a different plan since, I am now twenty-nine years old and in great health.

I have learned that we need to take God at His word. I have been fortunate to see the truths in this booklet lived out daily by the Jackson family, who have taught me and my family how to stand on the promises of God, how to pray with belief and expectancy, and how to receive healing by the blood of Jesus.

This booklet will not only teach you how to implement God's Word, but it will also teach you how to apply Scripture to overcome the enemy in various situations in your life. I have learned that praising and thanking God in every situation can be just as important as when we first go to Him with our prayer requests. When we take God at His word, we see His faithfulness surround our lives. Just watch what He can do!

Blessings!
Rachel M. Bunn

# The Word of God Gives Light

**Psalm 119:130:**

"The unfolding of your words gives light; it gives understanding to the simple [childlike].

**What two things does the Word of God give to the mind of the Christian?**

1. _____

2. _____

❖

**Answers:**
1. Light
2. Understanding


God's great gift to all men everywhere is His Word. It is the Word of life. Humbly acknowledged, it will produce in your life the fruits of God's corrective discipline, and will eventually lead you into His presence forever and ever.

As a family, we have come to believe that God's Word is our most treasured asset.

# LIFE COMES FROM THE WORD OF GOD

**Proverbs 4:20-22:**

> My son, pay attention to what I say; listen closely to my words. Do not let them out of your sight, keep them within your heart; for they are life to those who find them and health to a man's whole body.

**What are the three instructions that God gives His people through this proverb?**

1. _____

2. _____

3. _____

❖

**Answers:**

1. Pay attention. Listen closely to My words.
2. Do not let My words out of your sight.
3. Keep them within your heart.

**What will the result be?**

_____

❖

**Answer:**

Life and health to the whole body.

Proverbs is a book of "common sense." It tells us how to make the most of life and warns us that many people waste it. Its wisdom will enable us to arrive at the end of life and be pleased with what God has accomplished through our lives.

The question we all ask ourselves is: "How do I make time to read God's Word along with my other daily responsibilities?" One way is to keep verses of Scripture on a small card in your pocket or in a convenient place where you work. Make the mirrors in your bathroom and the refrigerator doors places where printed reminders of your faith can be read or quoted aloud.

## GOD'S WILL IS IN HIS WORD

The apostle John was probably in his eighties when he wrote this letter to us as a grandfather might write to his children and grandchildren. He was one of the twelve apostles called by Jesus during His earthly ministry, the only one to live to an old age. It is near the end of his earthly life that he offered this prayer for us:

**3 John 2:**

> Beloved, I wish above all things that thou mayest prosper and be in health, even as thy soul prospereth. (KJV)

**Above all things, what are the things God wants us to enjoy?**

1. _____

2. _____

3. _____

**Answers:**
1. To prosper
2. To be in health
3. Our souls (our minds) to prosper

Almost immediately after we received Jesus we would kneel daily at the foot of our bed and say, "Heavenly Father, please do not let us waste our lives."

George had a strong desire to see the boys grow up in a somewhat rural area of the nation. He wanted them to learn the value of work, to be responsible, and to receive an education that would allow them to provide for a family. George had enjoyed the challenge of working under one of the nation's finest equine veterinarians. However, he decided to leave the South Florida race track practice behind and do what he thought was best for the family.

For me this was a test. We had a dream house in Hollywood, Florida. We were surrounded by Christian friends. Even though we saw little of George, we all enjoyed life there. However, I had learned the importance of honoring your husband, and I knew without a doubt that it was something I must do without delay. I knew God expected me not only to move but to do it with joy. I sang from Florida to Tennessee to keep from crying.

We moved to Murfreesboro, bought acreage at the edge of town, and established an equine practice. With American Saddle Bred barns and Tennessee Walking Horse farms, there was no lack of work. We chose to build the clinic and live in the small house that was on the property.

Third John 2, the verse quoted on page 20, became real to us. We *believed* we could build a new house, and did so. Nothing is as rich and resourceful as the Word of God. Nothing is so fulfilling as believing and trusting God.

# CHAPTER THREE

# What Happened in the Beginning?

........................................................

## THE TEMPTATION AND THE FALL OF MAN

### Genesis 3:1-13

Now the serpent was more crafty than any of the
wild animals the LORD God had made. He said to
the woman, "Did God really say, 'You must not eat
from any tree in the garden'?"

The woman said to the serpent, "We may eat
fruit from the trees in the garden," but God did say,
"You must not eat fruit from the tree that is in the
middle of the garden, and you must not touch it, or
you will die.'"

"You will not surely die," the serpent said to the
woman. "For God knows that when you eat of it
your eyes will be opened, and you will be like God,
knowing good and evil."

When the woman saw that the fruit of the tree
was good for food and pleasing to the eye, and also

desirable for gaining wisdom, she took some and ate it. She also gave some to her husband, who was with her, and he ate it.

Then the eyes of both of them were opened, and they realized they were naked; so they sewed fig leaves together and made coverings for themselves.

Then the man and his wife heard the sound of the Lord God as he was walking in the garden in the cool of the day, and they hid from the Lord God among the trees of the garden. But the Lord God called to the man, "Where are you?"

He answered, "I heard you in the garden, and I was afraid because I was naked; so I hid."

And he said, "Who told you that you were naked? Have you eaten from the tree that I commanded you not to eat from?"

The man said, "The woman you put here with me—she gave me some fruit from the tree, and I ate it."

Then the LORD God said to the woman, "What is this you have done?" The woman said, "The serpent deceived me, and I ate."

1. Who deceived man? _____

2. Who accused God? _____

3. What was the result of their sin? _____
   _____

4. Whom does the man blame? _____

5. Whom does the woman blame? _____

**Answers:**

1. The great deceiver, the serpent (Satan), insinuated a falsehood and portrayed rebellion as clever.
2. Satan accuses God of having unworthy motives.
3. Adam and Eve were afraid of God. Their eyes were opened, but the result was quite different from what Satan had promised; fear entered their hearts.
4. The man blames God and the woman—anyone but himself—for his sin.
5. The woman blames the serpent rather than herself.

Adam and Eve possessed both eternal life and moral discernment as they came from the hand of God. Their access to the fruit of the tree of life showed that God's will and intention for them was life. In the eating of the fruit of the tree of knowledge of good and evil, Adam and Eve chose a creaturely source of discernment in order to be morally independent of God.

One important lesson to be learned from this account is that neither Adam nor Eve were willing to humble themselves and accept responsibility for their own part in the experience. Humbling yourself, accepting responsibility, and confessing your sin without blaming someone else is always a wise choice. We are dealing with an omniscient God.

**Hebrews 4:13b:**

> Everything is uncovered and laid bare before the eyes of him to whom we must give account.

**Adam and Eve disobeyed God. They made choices that would affect all people for all time. God's response:**

**Genesis 3:16-19:**

> To the woman he said, "I will greatly increase your pains in childbearing; with pain you will give birth to children. Your desire will be for your husband, and he will rule over you."
>
> To Adam he said, "Because you listened to your wife and ate from the tree about which I commanded you, 'You must not eat of it,' cursed is the ground because of you; through painful toil you will eat of it all the days of your life. It will produce thorns and thistles for you, and you will eat the plants of the field. By the sweat of your brow you will eat your food until you return to the ground, since from it you were taken; for dust you are and to dust you will return."

1. **What was the affect on woman of Adam and Eve's sin?**

   _____

2. **On man?** _____

3. **On every man and woman, boy and girl?**

   _____

   _____

**Answers:**

1. Pains in childbearing. Her judgment fell on what was most uniquely hers as a woman and as a suitable helper for her husband.
2. The man's "painful toil" was a judgment on him as worker of the soil. Though he would have to work hard and long (judgment), the man would be able to produce food that would sustain life (grace).
3. Death ("…and to dust you will return)." Man's labor would not be able to stave off death.

In disobedience man turned away from God, lost His protection and blessing, and came under a curse and the power of the devil. Yet, God made a way through Christ on the cross. He loves us and wants to bless us, to save us from sickness as well as sin.

# CHAPTER FOUR

# We Have an Enemy, Satan

..................................................

**John 10:10:**

> The thief [Satan] comes only to steal and kill and destroy; I [Jesus] have come that they may have life, and have it to the full.

1. **What three things does Satan come to do?**

   a. _____

   b. _____

   c. _____

2. **Why did Jesus come?** _____
   _____
   _____

**Answers:**

1. Satan comes to steal, kill, and destroy. His interest is in himself.
2. Jesus came to give us life on earth and in eternity. His interest is in all who follow Him in obedience.

The term *life* is used thirty-six times in the book of John. Following are a few examples:

"I give them eternal life, and they shall never perish" (10:28).

"I am the way and the truth and the life. No one comes to the Father except through me." (14:6).

"I am the light of the world. Whoever follows me will never walk in darkness, but will have the light of life" (8:12).

Learning this truth was a turning point for me. I established two facts:

1. Satan is my enemy, and he has a plan to kill me.
2. Jesus is my friend, and He has a plan to give me life to the full.

Day after day, I said, "Jesus, I believe that You love me and You are much stronger than any satanic force that will ever come against me."

# WHO AFFLICTED JOB?

## Job 2:7:

Satan went out from the presence of the LORD and afflicted Job with painful sores from the soles of his feet to the top of his head.

## Who brought this sickness? _____

❖

## Answer:

Satan

Job learned four things in the battle for his life on earth.
About God:
"I know that you can do all things; no plan of yours can be thwarted" (Job 42:2).
About Satan:
"He looks down on all that are haughty; he is king over all that are proud" (Job 41:34).

## What four things did Job learn?

1. _____
2. _____
3. _____
4. _____

**Answers:**

1. God can do all things.
2. God's plans cannot be thwarted.
3. Satan watches those who are haughty.
4. Satan is king over all who are proud.

## WHAT OPPRESSES US WITH SICKNESS?

**Acts 10:38:**

> God anointed Jesus of Nazareth with the Holy
> Spirit and power, and . . . he went around doing
> good and healing all who were under the power of
> the devil, because God was with him.

**What is it that oppresses us with sickness?**

_____

**Answer:**

The power of the devil.

I will always thank God for Lydia Prince, who refused to pray
for me when she recognized how frightened I was. There was
no doubt in my mind that Lydia loved me. Her response was
just what I needed to continue my journey through the
Scriptures. As I did so I learned that Jesus, time and again,
said to his followers, "Fear not." His words were frustrating to

me because the fear remained in my heart. Then I came to a passage in 1 John 4:18: "Perfect love drives out fear." It became clear to me how important it was to overcome fear, and my greater need was to love Jesus more and more. My prayer became, "God, help me to love You more." Second Timothy 1:7 became my constant companion: "God has not given us a spirit of fear, but of power and of love and of a sound mind. (NKJV)

It was not long before I noticed a marked difference in myself. The fearful thoughts that oppressed me were no longer there. Little by little, Jesus became the center of my thoughts, and I often go back to that lesson today.

For many years while I worked for George in the office of the veterinary clinic we had household help. Jesse was one of us; she worked in the house, which was within walking distance of the clinic, but she had a powerful fear. She had suffered a nervous breakdown some years before she came to work for us, and because of her fear she wanted Doyle, who was four years old at that time, to remain in the house with her. This went on for several months until one day Doyle grew weary of her demands. He crawled up on a chair and reached to the top of the bookshelf for the children's Bible. Opening it, he turned to a picture of Jesus and said to Jesse, "Who is that, Jesse?"

"Jesus," she answered.

He then turned the pages until he came to a picture of Satan. "Now Jesse, who is that?"

"Satan," she replied.

"Who is the most powerful?" he asked.

"Jesus, of course," she said.

"Then I am going out to play, and you need never be afraid again," he answered.

From that day on, Doyle had the freedom to go out of doors and Jesse remained comfortable alone in the house.

## A Crippled Woman

**Luke 13:11, 16:**

> A woman was there who had been crippled by a spirit for eighteen years. She was bent over and could not straighten up at all . . . .
>
> [Jesus said,] "Then should not this woman, a daughter of Abraham, whom Satan has kept bound for eighteen long years, be set free on the Sabbath day from what bound her?"

**Who brought sickness on this woman?**

_____

**Answer:**
She had been crippled by a spirit from Satan.

# CHAPTER FIVE

# Witchcraft and the Occult

......................................................

Witchcraft involves acknowledging and/or worshipping false gods. God's judgment on the breaking of the following two commandments bears the characteristic mark of a curse. It continues from generation to generation, at least as far as the fourth generation. These two sins dominate America and the world we live in today. In some nations the practice of worshipping false gods goes back hundreds and even thousands of years.

**Exodus 20:1-6:**

> And God spoke all these words, saying:
> "I am the LORD your God, who brought you out of the land of Egypt, out of the house of bondage.
> You shall have no other gods before Me.
> You shall not make for yourself a carved image—any likeness of anything that is in heaven above, or that is in the earth beneath, or that is in the water under the earth; you shall not bow down to them

nor serve them. For I, the LORD your God, am a jealous God, visiting the iniquity [sin and consequences of sin] of the fathers upon the children to the third and fourth generations of those who hate Me." (NKJV)

## Romans 1:20-23:

Since the creation of the world His invisible attributes are clearly seen, being understood by the things that are made, even His eternal power and Godhead, so that they are without excuse, because, although they knew God, they did not glorify Him as God, nor were thankful, but became futile in their thoughts, and their foolish hearts were darkened. Professing to be wise, they became fools, and changed the glory of the incorruptible God into an image made like corruptible man—and birds and four-footed animals and creeping things. (NKJV)

**What are the two sins that bring punishment to the third and fourth generations?**

1. _____

   _____

2. _____

   _____

**Answers:**
1. Acknowledging any other god before—or besides—the Lord. We must acknowledge that He is the only true God. There is no other.
2. Making any artificial representation of God and offering worship to it.

Participation in any group that denies that Jesus Christ is Lord and/or elevates any teaching or book to the level of the Bible must be renounced (Examples: Christian Science, Church of Scientology, Free Masonry, Hinduism, Islam, Jehovah's Witness, Mormonism, and the list goes on). Likewise, any group that requires dark, secret initiations, ceremonies, vows, pacts, or covenants must also be renounced. Those who trespass in this area seek from Satan the supernatural knowledge or power that God does not permit man to seek from any other source but Himself.

**Faith's Response:** Heavenly Father, I acknowledge that I have sinned against You by seeking supernatural knowledge through false gods. I ask You to forgive me, and release me from the curse that is pronounced on those who break the first commandment. I thank You that You do forgive me. In Jesus name, amen.

## THE OCCULT

Two of the strongest cravings of human nature are the desire for knowledge and the desire for power. If a man cannot satisfy these cravings through natural sources and natural means, he will inevitably turn to supernatural sources. It is at this point that he easily becomes entrapped in the occult. Witchcraft is an expression of man's rebellion against God. It is an attempt for man to gain his own ends without submitting to God's ways. Its driving force is a desire to control people and circumstances by intimidation and manipulation for the purpose of domination.

## 1 Samuel 15:23:

> Rebellion is as the sin of witchcraft, and stubbornness is as iniquity and idolatry. (NKJV)

## What two sins open us to witchcraft and idolatry?

1. _____

2. _____

**Answers:**
1. Rebellion against God.
2. Stubbornness.

## Deuteronomy 18:10-13:

> There shall not be found among you anyone who makes his son or his daughter pass through the fire, or one who practices witchcraft, or a soothsayer, or one who interprets omens, or a sorcerer, or one who conjures spells, or a medium, or a spiritist, or one who calls up the dead. For all who do these things are an abomination to the LORD, and because of these abominations the LORD your God drives them out

from before you. You shall be blameless before the LORD your God. (NKJV)

If you have been involved at any time in such activities or practices, you have crossed an invisible border into the kingdom of Satan. Since the kingdom of God and the kingdom of Satan are in total opposition to each other, you cannot enjoy the full rights and benefits of a citizenship in God's kingdom until you have finally and forever severed all connection with Satan and totally canceled any claim he may have against you.

**Acts 19:18-19:**

> Many of those who believed now came and openly confessed their evil deeds. A number who had practiced sorcery brought their scrolls together and burned them publicly. When they calculated the value of the scrolls, the total came to fifty thousand drachmas. [A drachma was a silver coin worth about a day's wages.]

Have you ever been hypnotized, involved with satanic rituals, Yoga, séances/mediums/channelers, or been to a fortuneteller or had your palm read? Have you played with a Ouija board, tarot cards, or a magic eight ball? The list goes on. If so, we urge you to pray the following prayer.

**Faith's Response:** In the name of Jesus, I renounce all contact with anything occult or satanic. If I have any "contact objects," I commit myself to destroy them. I cancel all of Satan's claims against me. I now open myself to receive Your blessing in every way You want to impart it to me.

# CHAPTER SIX

# The Question of Faith

## DO YOU BELIEVE?

**Romans 10:9-10:**

> If you confess with your mouth, "Jesus is Lord," and believe in your heart that God raised him from the dead, you will be saved. For it is with your heart that you believe and are justified, and it is with your mouth that you confess and are saved.

**What two things are required of us to "be saved" from our old way of life and to begin a new life?**

1. _____

2. _____

**Answers:**
1. Confess out loud that Jesus is Lord.
2. Believe in our heart that God raised Him from the dead.

**Faith's Response:**
Lord Jesus Christ, I believe that You are the Son of God and the only way to God; and that You died on the cross for my sins and rose again from the dead. I give up all my rebellion and all my sin, and I submit myself to You as my Lord.

On our knees around the coffee table in our Sunday school teacher's living room we prayed this prayer, and our lives were radically changed. We bought a New Testament, began to read it, and attended a "small group" where we had discussion and prayer together with like-minded Christ followers on a regular basis.

One of our favorite prayers is "We are God's workmanship, created in Christ Jesus to do good works, which God prepared in advance for us to do" (Ephesians 2:10).

## FAITH INCREASED

**Romans 10:17:**

> Faith comes from hearing, and hearing by the word of Christ. (NASB)

**How does faith come?**

_____

**Answer:**

Faith comes as we hear the word of Christ.

### Romans 10:17:

> The point is, Before you trust, you have to listen. But unless Christ's Word is preached, there's nothing to listen to. (*The Message*)

### How do we learn to trust God?

---

**Answer:**

Trust is a decision, and it comes when we decide to listen.

To be a Christian is to trust Jesus as your Savior and Lord. It involves learning to trust God as a person, and to gain confidence in His character and His faithfulness. The newest Christ follower has this faith. The love that God pours into our hearts when we turn to Him and invite Him into our lives is so great, nothing we have ever experienced can compare to it.

At one point, we struggled with the question: Do I have faith? This passage of Scripture changed our thinking:

> I am crucified with Christ: nevertheless I live; yet not I, but Christ liveth in me: and the life which I now live in the flesh I live by the faith of the Son of God, who loved me, and gave himself for me. (Galatians 2:20 KJV)

We knew then, it is not only by our faith we live, but by His faithfulness:

> This God is our God for ever and ever; he will be our guide even to the end. (Psalm 48:14)

## GOD REQUIRES OBEDIENCE

**Exodus 15:26:**

> If you listen carefully to the voice of the LORD your God and do what is right in his eyes, if you pay attention to his commands and keep all his decrees, I will not bring on you any of the diseases I brought on the Egyptians, for I am the LORD, who heals you.

**What does God promise to do for His people who obey Him?**

_____

_____

**Answer:**
God promises not to bring any of the diseases He brought on the Egyptians.

The covenant between God and Israel at Mount Sinai is the outgrowth and extension of the Lord's covenant with Abraham and his descendants six hundred years earlier.

Participation in the divine blessings is conditioned on obedience added to faith.

The equivalent phrases used by Christians are found in 1 Peter 2:9:

> You are a chosen people, a royal priesthood, a holy nation, a people belonging to God, that you may declare the praises of him who called you out of darkness into his wonderful light.

## FORGIVENESS

### Matthew 6:14-15:

> If you forgive men when they sin against you, your heavenly Father will also forgive you. But if you do not forgive men their sins, your Father will not forgive your sins.

**What two promises are made in this passage?**

1.  _____

2.  _____

**Answers:**
1. If we forgive men who sin against us, God will forgive us.
2. If we do not forgive men their sins, God will not forgive us.

In our years of counseling, we have found unforgiveness to be one of the most common sources of frustration in one's spiritual life as well as the cause for an apparent failure to receive answers to prayer. Many times there is only one specific person whom we need to forgive.

- Forgiveness is not forgetting. People who try to forget find that they cannot.
- Forgetting may be a result of forgiveness, but it is never the means of forgiveness.
- Forgiveness deals with your pain, not another's behavior.
- Forgiveness does not mean that you agree with the person you are forgiving. Remember: Positive feelings will follow in time; freeing yourself from the past is the critical issue.

List the names of the persons who have offended you. Describe in writing how they made you feel. Name the specific wrongs you have suffered:

- rejection
- physical, verbal, sexual or emotional abuse
- deprivation of love
- injustice
- unfairness
- neglect and/or betrayal

Those closest to us are the ones who have the power to hurt us the most—father, mother, spouse, children, and friends. Sometimes we hold false expectations of God that lead us to anger or bitterness toward Him. For our own good we need to ask God to forgive us for being angry with Him and for our wrong expectations and feelings toward Him. Some of us need to forgive ourselves for weaknesses and sins that God has long since forgiven. It might help you to make a list of perceived slights, sins, or weaknesses, then tear it up.

Jesus limits us. He said in Mark 11:25: "Whenever you stand praying, if you have anything against anyone, forgive him, that your Father in heaven may also forgive you your trespasses" (NKJV).

**Faith's Response:** By a decision of my will, I forgive all who have harmed me or wronged me just as I want God to forgive me. I especially forgive _____, _____, and _____ completely. In Jesus' name, amen.

## OVERCOMING BITTERNESS

Early summer days were filled with the veterinary clinic operating at full capacity.

The pastures were home to many broodmares and foals. Newborns sometimes needed to be bottle-fed throughout the night and this required the attention not only of George, but usually one of the boys as well. Owners were calling from various states to get a detailed description of the new foal or the reproductive status of their mare. It was a busy and exciting time.

One particular morning, a friend asked us to visit a good friend and coworker who was in the hospital with a serious illness. Even with the best possible medical care, her body refused to heal. We had not met the woman, but we agreed to go immediately.

At the edge of our patio the rose garden was full of bright blossoms; we cut some roses, arranged them in a silver vase, and went to the room where the lady our friend had described was waiting. She was desperate. Advanced breast cancer had required a double mastectomy several days earlier.

Her story was like so many. We learned that she had suffered a great disappointment in her marriage and had not overcome the anger and resentment it had caused. Some years earlier, she and her husband had agreed on a plan for their future. He would take a job that required his being far from home. She would remain in middle Tennessee, continuing her career and responsibilities to the children. At a set time he would retire, and they would have the money to build their dream home free of debt.

Shortly after his retirement he arrived back in Tennessee. But he told his wife he had given the money he had agreed to save to a woman with whom he had had a lengthy affair. When he told her, she said, "I want to die!" They continued to live together. She loved her husband and did not want a divorce, but she was full of bitterness. We assured her that we would search the Scriptures and come back very soon to give her a report on what we had learned.

As we returned to the back door of our house, I heard these words: "You too have bitterness." I knew in my heart that these words were true, and I needed to study what the Bible said about it for my own sake as well as for our newfound friend.

We all have cause for bitterness, and this verse from the book of Hebrews offers a good lesson.

> Look after each other so that not one of you will fail to find God's best blessings. Watch out that no bitterness take root among you, for as it springs up it causes deep trouble, hurting many in their spiritual lives. (12:15 TLB)

When we returned to the hospital with a handful of roses for the silver vase and a copy of *The Living Bible*, she made a decision to repent of the bitterness that she had allowed to grow in her own heart. Even though she had been a Sunday school teacher, she realized that she had never really received Jesus as her Savior, but had been trying to live in her own strength. She prayed to receive Jesus and to forgive herself for the bitterness she harbored. She also prayed to forgive the man she loved, and to be free of the curse she had brought on herself when she said, "I want to die." Her body immediately began to heal. In the following twenty years, this woman was able to help many other women overcome bitterness.

## CORRIE TEN BOOM: LOVE YOUR ENEMY

In her book *Tramp for the Lord*, Corrie ten Boom recounts coming face-to-face with one of the most cruel guards of Ravensbruck, the concentration camp she and her sister, Betsie, were confined to, and where Betsie had died. She had just finished giving a gospel message to a gathering of people when the man approached her:

> Now he was in front of me, hand thrust out: . . . "You mentioned Ravensbruck in your talk," he was saying. "I was a guard there." No, he did not remember me.
>
> "But since that time," he went on, "I have become a Christian. I know that God has forgiven me for the cruel things I did there, but I would like to hear it from your lips as well. Fraulein,"—again the hand came out—"will you forgive me?"

The seconds that ticked by "seemed hours" as Corrie wrestled with "the most difficult things [she] ever had to do."

Finally, after recalling Jesus' teachings concerning forgiveness,

woodenly, mechanically, I thrust my hand into the one stretched out to me. And as I did, an incredible thing took place. The current started in my shoulder, raced down my arm, sprang into our joined hands. And then this healing warmth seemed to flood my whole being, bringing tears to my eyes.

"I forgive you, brother!" I cried. "With all my heart."

For a long moment we grasped each other's hands, the former guard and the former prisoner. I had never known God's love so intensely, as I did then. But even so, I realized it was not my love. I had tried, and did not have the power. It was the power of the Holy Spirit as recorded in Romans 5:5, ". . . because the love of God is shed abroad in our hearts by the Holy Ghost which is given unto us."

## FAITH TESTED

It was a Saturday, a hot summer day in 1971. The family had taken a day to fast and pray together, a common practice for us. We were asking God for His help in planning a prayer service for our nation. It was to be held at the National Guard Armory in downtown Nashville. Derek and Lydia were coming from Florida, as Derek would be speaking; and our good friends from Philadelphia, Melvin and Evelyn Simpson, were arriving to provide music and lead worship for the special event.

In the afternoon, the three boys had joined George on a tractor drive along the creek of our small farm. As they returned to the clinic, the boys were standing on the drawbar of the tractor. When they came to a gate in order to get back out of the field, Allen jumped off the bar to open the gate. George sped up the tractor, pretending to run away from Allen. Phillip was very amused by it, and laughed so hard that, without his noticing, his foot was moving toward the tractor tire. The wheel caught Phillip's leg and threw him up over the tractor and to the ground, trapping his leg. Allen and Doyle were screaming to get George's attention, when suddenly he stopped the tractor. Doyle, who was four years old at the time, put his hands on his hips, turned his face toward the sky and spoke in a loud voice, "God, we need You right here, right now." George instantly thought to remove the air from the tractor tire and was able to pull Phillip's leg free.

As George laid Phillip on the car seat he heard the bones crepitate, indicating a fracture. The local hospital was notified that we were in route with an emergency. One of us said to Phillip: "Say this Scripture from Isaiah 53:5: 'He was wounded for our transgressions, He was bruised for our iniquities . . .and by His stripes we are healed.'" (NKJV) Phillip did not say that, but instead prayed aloud in his own prayer language.

When we arrived at the hospital a few minutes later, three doctors were waiting in the emergency room—Dr. James Garrison, our pediatrician, along with a surgeon and a radiologist. X-rays were ordered immediately. Then all three doctors returned from the emergency room with Phillip on a stretcher. The report was simple: "There is no fracture." George instantly raised his hands and praised God. Each doctor wiped his eyes, and then the radiologist said, "We must take him back for a second set of X-rays to be certain."

In a very few minutes the report came back in Phillip's favor: "No broken bones."

Phillip was left with a large pressure ulcer that caused a contracted tendon in his leg. For the next six months he walked with a marked limp. Surgery was scheduled over the coming Easter holiday. As a family, we thanked God daily for Phillip's healing. Six months passed with no change.

We learned that Kenneth Hagin was to speak on a Sunday afternoon in Chattanooga, and we made plans to attend the meeting. Kenneth Hagin gave a message, and then asked those who had believed God for an answer to a specific prayer to stand. "I want to agree with you," he said.

Phillip was standing next to George. Our family of five stood together holding hands. Before Kenneth Hagin prayed, Phillip began to weep and looked up into his dad's face. "Daddy, my leg felt warm and jumped," he said. When George checked further, Phillip's foot was flat on the floor; God had heard our prayer. No surgery was required. God is always happy to hear His children pray, and He is often quick to answer them.

# CHAPTER SEVEN

# Entering the Presence of God

·······················································

## ENTERING GOD'S PRESENCE

**Psalm 100:4:**

> Enter his gates with thanksgiving and his courts with praise; give thanks to him and praise his name.

**How does the psalmist say we come before God?**

1. _____

2. _____

**Answers:**
1. Thanksgiving (thanking Him for who He is).
2. Praise (praising Him for His greatness!).

Being willing to praise God is a choice we make. It becomes the condition of our hearts. Praise is vocal; it is uttered. Our God is great—great in mercy, great in love, great in power, great in creative works, great in His dealings with us.

Praising God for His greatness makes you God-centered, lifts you out of yourself, and brings you into contact with the one who can completely transform your life.

## PRAISE THE LORD

**Psalm 103:2-4:**

> Praise the LORD, O my soul, and forget not all his benefits—who forgives all your sins and heals all your diseases, who redeems your life from the pit and crowns you with love and compassion.

**List the personal benefits we receive from the Lord:**

1. _____

2. _____

3. _____

4. _____

**Answers:**
1. Forgiveness of sins.
2. Healing from diseases.
3. Redeems our lives from the pit.
4. Crowns us with love and compassion.

# CHAPTER EIGHT

# Jesus
# of Nazareth

·······························································

## JESUS IN THE SYNAGOGUE AT NAZARETH
## (ONE YEAR AFTER HIS MINISTRY BEGAN)

### Luke 4:14-21:

Jesus returned to Galilee in the power of the Spirit, and news about him spread through the whole countryside. He taught in their synagogues, and everyone praised him.

He went to Nazareth, where he had been brought up, and on the Sabbath day he went into the synagogue, as was his custom. And he stood up to read. The scroll of the prophet Isaiah was handed to him. Unrolling it, he found the place where it is written:

"The Spirit of the Lord is on me, because he has anointed me [not with literal oil, but with the Holy Spirit[ to preach good news to the poor. He has sent me to proclaim freedom for the prisoners and recovery of sight for the blind, to release the oppressed, to proclaim the year of the Lord's favor."

Then he rolled up the scroll [of the prophet Isaiah] gave it back to the attendant and sat down. The eyes of everyone in the synagogue were fastened on him, and he began by saying to them, "Today this scripture is fulfilled in your hearing."

# JESUS ON THE CROSS -
# THE MESSAGE OF MERCY FOR ALL WHO RECEIVE IT

## Foretold by the Prophet Isaiah (53:4-5):

Surely he took up our infirmities and carried our sorrows, yet we considered him stricken by God, smitten by him, and afflicted.

But he was pierced for our transgressions, he was crushed for our iniquities; the punishment that brought us peace was upon him, and by his wounds we are healed.

## What was the purpose of Christ's death on the cross?

1. _____

2. _____

3. _____

4. _____

5. _____

6. _____

**Answers:**

1. He took our infirmities (literally sicknesses).
2. He carried our sorrows (literally pains).
3. He was pierced for our transgressions (breaking a law or commandment).
4. He was crushed for our iniquities (lack of righteousness, justice; or wickedness).
5. He was punished that we might have peace.
6. He was wounded that we would be healed.

**Matthew 8:17:**

> This was to fulfill what was spoken through the prophet Isaiah: "He took up our infirmities and carried our diseases."

**1 Peter 2:24:**

> He himself bore our sins in his body on the tree, so that we might die to sins and live for righteousness; by his wounds you have been healed.

## WHY DID JESUS COME TO EARTH?

**1 John 3:8:**

> He who does what is sinful is of the devil, because the devil has been sinning from the beginning. The reason the Son of God appeared was to destroy the devil's work.

## Why did Jesus come to earth?

**Answer:**
To destroy the devil's work.

The apostle John is not asserting sinless perfection; rather, he's explaining that the believer's life is characterized not by sin but by doing what is right.

The devil has sinned since he first rebelled against God, before the fall of Adam and Eve. He is the instigator of human sin, and those who continue to sin belong to him and are his children.

### John 8:44:

> You belong to your father, the devil, and you want to carry out your father's desire. He was a murderer from the beginning, not holding to the truth, for there is no truth in him. When he lies, he speaks his native language, for he is a liar and the father of lies.

# CHAPTER NINE

# Jesus Came for Broken Hearts

...........................................................................

Jesus came for broken lives and broken hearts, which often leave us with feelings of rejection.

**Isaiah 61:1-3:**

> He has sent me to bind up the brokenhearted, . . . to comfort all who mourn, and provide for those who grieve in Zion—to bestow on them a crown of beauty instead of ashes, the oil of gladness instead of mourning, and a garment of praise instead of a spirit of despair.

**What will God do for the brokenhearted and for those who mourn or grieve?**

1. _____

2. _____

3. _____

4. _____

**Answers:**
1. He will bind up the brokenhearted.
2. He will comfort all who mourn.
3. He will provide for those who grieve.
4. He will bestow on those who grieve a crown of beauty instead of ashes, the oil of gladness instead of mourning, and a garment of praise instead of a spirit of despair.

Jesus is acquainted with broken hearts; at the time of His own death, He Himself cried out to God from a broken heart. Jesus was rejected that we might be accepted by God; He understands the pain of rejection.

**Matthew 27:46:**

> About the ninth hour Jesus cried out with a loud voice, saying, "My God, My God, why have You forsaken Me?" (NKJV)

**Isaiah 53:3:**

> He was despised and rejected by men, a man of sorrows, and familiar with suffering. Like one from whom men hide their faces he was despised, and we esteemed him not.

# Broken Heart Healed

Mark S. Josovitz, M.D., gives the following testimony:

Born and raised an Orthodox Jew in New Jersey, an hour and fifteen minutes from New York City, I studied in Hebrew school, and for a period attended an Orthodox Jewish school in Miami Beach. My father was a Holocaust survivor whose wife and daughter were killed in the Holocaust. My father was fifty and my mother thirty-eight, I was three days old when they adopted me. I loved them both dearly. As most Jewish parents, they believed in a strong education: study, study, study—both in English and in Hebrew school.

I was engaged, and my Christian fiancée, Dee Dee DeWitt, was always happy and filled with joy. There was a glow about her. She introduced me to Jesus, a very strange topic to me. Not being a part of my childhood training, I knew nothing about the New Testament. In June of 2000 we were in the Titans stadium in Nashville where Billy Graham gave the gospel message. I found it to be inspirational, enlightening, and heartwarming. I accepted Jesus the Messiah that night and experienced a fulfillment I had never known before. In December of that same year we were married. I have a daughter, Sarah, by a previous marriage; we now have another daughter, Sophie.

Two years after our marriage, at the age of forty-seven, I found myself in the pit of despair. I had reverted back to a life of living for the world and my own fleshly desires. After losing everything that was most important to me, I found myself out of work as a medical doctor and without my family. I had fallen so hard, so fast, I didn't have a friend to my name. I felt a hopeless failure, with no desire to practice medicine. I was a broken man with a broken heart.

Through my despair God extended a lifeline. I found a tangible expression of God's love through my church. In my desperation I determined to yield to God. I am a changed man. These believers never rejected me. I love them for that. George and Betty Jackson helped me to process right and wrong behaviors. They did not judge. My family was completely restored and made better than in the beginning. I reentered practice with a daily consciousness that my healing was a product of spiritual change and must be sustained by my daily life.

God has taken me from the overwhelming depths of hopelessness and depression to experiencing the glorious light of His restorative goodness. I find my greatest asset for the present is my past because of the blood of Jesus.

I regularly see patients who have chronic conditions that are joined to a spiritual need in their life. When they are spiritually healthy they are able to respond to treatment and may no longer require medication. This is usually a circumstance I can't explain, but by my own experience, I understand. My life has been a vivid example. I have learned about healing that involves spirit, soul, and body.

# PERSONAL APPLICATION OF THE CROSS

**1 Peter 2:24:**

> He himself bore our sins in His body on the tree, so
> that we might die to sins and live for righteousness;
> by His wounds you have been healed.

**How do you apply in your life the finished work of the cross of Jesus?**

---

**Answer:**

Recognizing that the answer is not in you, but in Jesus.

When you struggle with fear, pain, depression, or discouragement, memorize this or other applicable passages of Scripture. The most powerful thing you can do is to turn to the Word of God and away from yourself. Look to Him.

You may be in a battle for your life, for your marriage, for a child, or for a parent. Whatever the case may be, it is a battle! The battle rages in one's mind. For me, as a working mother, I would write out a Scripture and fasten it in some way to whatever I was wearing. Throughout the day, when I was alone, I would read it aloud until it was firmly fixed in my mind.

Dreams can be frightening. Before going to bed, declare God's protection over you while you sleep. You will be amazed what a difference this makes.

**2 Corinthians 10:3-5:**

> Though we live in the world, we do not wage war as the world does. The weapons we fight with are not the weapons of the world. On the contrary, they have divine power to demolish strongholds. We demolish arguments and every pretension that sets itself up against the knowledge of God, and we take captive every thought to make it obedient to Christ.

Don't allow the enemy to convince you that you cannot control your mind.

## THE HEALING MINISTRY OF JESUS

**Matthew 4:23:** "Jesus went throughout Galilee, teaching in their synagogues, preaching the good news of the kingdom, and healing every disease and sickness among the people."

**Matthew 8:2-3:** "A man with leprosy came and knelt before him and said, 'Lord, if you are willing, you can make me clean.' Jesus reached out his hand and touched the man. 'I am willing,' he said. 'Be clean!' Immediately he was cured of his leprosy."

**Matthew 9:2, 6:** "Some men brought to him a paralytic, lying on a mat. When Jesus saw their faith, he said to the paralytic, 'Take heart, son; your sins are forgiven.' . . . Then he said to the paralytic, 'Get up, take your mat and go home.'"

**Matthew 9:35:** "Jesus went through all the towns and villages, teaching in their synagogues, preaching the good news of the kingdom and healing every disease and sickness."

**Matthew 14:35-36:** "When the men of that place recognized Jesus, they sent word to all the surrounding country. People brought all their sick to him and begged him to let the sick just touch the edge of his cloak, and all who touched him were healed."

**Matthew 15:30:** "Great crowds came to him, bringing the lame, the blind, the crippled, the mute and many others, and laid them at his feet; and he healed them."

**Matthew 21:14:** "The blind and the lame came to him at the temple, and he healed them."

**Luke 17:11-14:** "On his way to Jerusalem, Jesus traveled along the border between Samaria and Galilee. As he was going into a village, ten men who had leprosy met him. They stood at a distance and called out in a loud voice, 'Jesus, Master, have pity on us!' When he saw them, he said, 'Go, show yourselves to the priests.' And as they went, they were cleansed."

**Luke 22:50-51:** "One of them struck the servant of the high priest, cutting off his right ear. But Jesus answered, 'No more of this!' And he touched the man's ear and healed him."

# God Does Not Change

**Malachi 3:6-7:** "'I the LORD do not change . . . . Return to me, and I will return to you', says the Lord Almighty."

**Hebrews 13:8:** "Jesus Christ is the same yesterday and today and forever."

**James 1:17:** "Every good and perfect gift is from above, coming down from the Father of the heavenly lights, who does not change like shifting shadows."

# CHAPTER TEN

# Jesus:
# The Lamb of God

∙∙∙∙∙∙∙∙∙∙∙∙∙∙∙∙∙∙∙∙∙∙∙∙∙∙∙∙∙∙∙∙∙∙∙∙∙∙∙∙∙∙∙∙∙∙∙∙∙∙∙∙∙∙∙∙∙∙∙∙∙∙∙∙∙∙∙∙∙∙∙∙∙

During the late sixties, we invested in video equipment and went throughout the middle Tennessee area to churches, home bible studies, and conferences showing the teachings of Derek Prince. One Sunday evening in a local church, George was showing the film *God's Atomic Weapon*. I felt so discouraged in my battle against cancer that I sat quietly and alone in the back of the sanctuary. But when they began viewing the tape, I made an outline of what was taught. We typed the outline and mailed it to Derek and Lydia Prince, who were then living in Ft. Lauderdale, Florida. At that time, their daughter Elizabeth was their only office employee. Derek's books (The Foundation Series) were being mailed across the nation. Soon after that, a copy of the outline, which is the following prayer, was included in the book orders. Coupled with the knowledge of our Passover Lamb, *The Blood of Jesus Confession* has become a weapon against the satanic forces for thousands of people all over the world.

# Jesus, Our Passover Lamb

The whole of Israel's deliverance out of Egypt centered in the Passover lamb. On the tenth day of the first month, every household was to choose a lamb. On the evening of the fourteenth day, the lamb was to be slain. Protection would come only through the blood of the lamb applied on the outside of the door of every Israelite's home in Egypt. God said, **"When I see the blood on your door, I will pass over you, the destroyer will not be allowed to come in"** (see Exodus 12:13, 23).

When the lamb was slain, the account makes it perfectly clear that the blood was carefully captured, drop by drop, in a basin. So the blood was in the basin—available but of no use. The blood in the basin was no protection. The blood had to be transferred from the basin to the door.

God gave them one, and only one, authorized means to do that. He instructed them to take a bunch of hyssop, a little herb that grows commonly all over the Middle East, and to dip the hyssop in the blood. When the hyssop was dripping with blood, they were to use it to smite the lintel and the two doorposts. In this way, the blood was transferred by the hyssop to the door. The hyssop, though it was such a humble thing, was an essential part of the total plan of deliverance. (see Exodus 12:22.)

When we apply this by analogy to our salvation in Christ, we note that Paul says in 1 Corinthians 5:7: **"Christ, our Passover lamb, has been sacrificed."** He has been killed. His blood has been shed. In the terms of the analogy, the blood is now in the basin. But the basin does nothing for you and me.

We have to transfer the blood from the basin to the place where we are—to our personal, spiritual, physical, financial, family, and business needs. Whatever it may be, we have to transfer the blood of Jesus out of the basin and to our lives. God has provided a means. Of course, it is not hyssop. What is it? It is by our testimony that we transfer the blood from the basin to the door. They overcame the evil one by the blood of the lamb and the word of their testimony.

## BY THE BLOOD OF THE LAMB AND THE WORD OF MY TESTIMONY! I OVERCOME THE DEVIL

**Revelation 12:11:**

> They [the believers on earth] overcame him [Satan] by the blood of the Lamb and by the word of their testimony, and they did not love their lives to the death. (NKJV)

**I, _____, testify to Satan personally as to what the Word of God says the blood of Jesus does for me.**

**Ephesians 1:7:** "In Him [that is, in Christ] we have redemption through His blood, the forgiveness of sins according to the riches of His grace" (NKJV).

**Psalm 107:2:** "Let the redeemed of the LORD say so, whom He has redeemed from the hand of the enemy" (NKJV).

The Bible tells us that:

- *Through the blood of Jesus, I am redeemed out of the hand of the devil.*

- *Through the blood of Jesus, all my sins are forgiven.*

**1 John 1:7:** "If we walk in the light as He [Jesus] is in the light, we have fellowship with one another, and the blood of Jesus Christ. His Son cleanses us from all sin" (NKJV).

- *The blood of Jesus Christ, God's Son, continually cleanses me from all sin.*

**Romans 5:9:** "Since we have now been justified by his blood, how much more shall we be saved from God's wrath through him!"

- *Through the blood of Jesus, I am justified, made righteous, just as if I'd never sinned.*

**Hebrews 13:12:** "Jesus also, that he might sanctify the people with his own blood, suffered outside the gate" (NKJV).

- *Through the blood of Jesus, I am sanctified, made holy, set apart to God.*

**1 Corinthians 6:13:** "The body is not for sexual immorality, but for the Lord, and the Lord for the body."

**1 Corinthians 6:19-20:** "Do you not know that your body is a temple of the Holy Spirit who is in you, whom you have from God, and you are not your own? For you were bought at a price; therefore glorify God in your body and in your spirit, which are God's" (NKJV).

**Faith's Response:** My body is a temple of the Holy Spirit, redeemed, cleansed, and sanctified by the blood of Jesus; therefore, because of all that has gone before, Satan has no place in me, no power over me through the blood of Jesus Christ. I renounce him, loose myself from him, and command him to leave me in the name of Jesus.

# The Prayer of Relinquishment

..........................................................................

## A SURRENDER OF MY WILL TO HIS WILL

In my ongoing struggle against cancer, which seemed to produce very few results, I often found myself approaching God with my list of wants and reminding Him that I did not want to leave my little boys motherless. "I love George and I want to live and be his wife," I would pray. It became clear to me that my strong will in this case was not to my benefit. It was in voicing these wants that I learned what a prayer of relinquishment meant.

What Jesus told His disciples in Luke 9 reveal what He required of me:

> If anyone would come after me, he must deny himself and take up his cross daily and follow me. For whoever wants to save his life will lose it, but whoever loses his life for me will save it. What good is it for a man to gain the whole world, and yet lose

or forfeit his very self? If anyone is ashamed of me and my words, the Son of Man will be ashamed of him when he comes in his glory and in the glory of the Father and of the holy angels. (verses 23-26)

I made the choice to pray and repeated it to Him aloud for a time. Then one evening to my surprise, I heard myself say, "Jesus, I love You more than George, I love You more than the boys, I love You more than myself. I want to do whatever You want me to do. If You want me to die of cancer, then that is exactly what I want."

The words of Jesus in John 11:25 had changed my life:

I am the resurrection and the life. He who believes in me will live, even though he dies; and whoever lives and believes in me will never die.

By the following day, the lumps were gone and have never returned.

**Faith's Response:** Heavenly Father, I thank You for loving me so much that You would die for me, that I might live for You and follow You all the days of my life. In Jesus' name, amen.

CPSIA information can be obtained at www.ICGtesting.com
Printed in the USA
LVOW11s0345040616

490888LV00001B/3/P